Seven Days to Higher Ground

A Devotional for Embracing a New Life

By Rebecca Benston

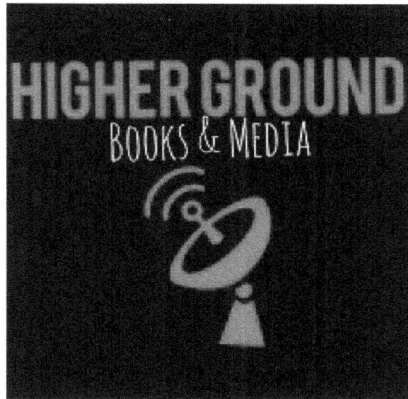

Scripture taken from the HOLY BIBLE, NEW INTERNATIONAL VERSION®. NIV®. Copyright © 1973, 1978, 1984 by International Bible Society. Used by permission of Zondervan. All rights reserved worldwide.

Higher Ground Books & Media
Springfield, Ohio.
http://www.highergroundbooksandmedia.com

Printed in the United States of America 2020

Foreword

The journey toward wholeness can be an extremely long and daunting one. What I've found most helpful as I stumbled along the path was a firm foundation in Christ and the many great resources that I've been able to find in the form of devotionals, online sermons, and education about Christianity. It's not all about crying out your sorrows and admitting defeat while wallowing helplessly in brokenness and praying that God will just fix the thing once and for all. But that's the mistaken idea I had when I set out to be a Christian. Thankfully, by continuing to seek the truth instead of settling for some myth of absolution and a dumbed-down, microwave version of what Jesus taught, I finally found what I needed to be able to face life's challenges with confidence and virtually no fear. Am I still scared sometimes? Of course, I am human. But more often than not, I am now able to stand tall in spite of that fear with the knowledge that after all is said and done, we win.

We are not stuck in one place unless we choose to be. God has shown me this time after time and thankfully, He continues to prove me wrong when I start to tell myself I can't do something. I hope that you will find inspiration in what I share throughout this devotional. These pages hold a combination of Scripture, recommendations for powerful worship music and sermons to empower you and to strengthen you as you build your relationship with God and make your way to Higher Ground with Him.

May God richly bless you and keep you! Carry on.

Rebecca Benston

How to use this book…

For each day, you'll see that there are basically three sections:

> An introduction paragraph,
> A verse of Scripture, and
> A brief bit of commentary about the verse which may or
> may not include references to resources that will be
> helpful to you as you work your way through the book.

Because I'm the type of person who has difficulty sticking to a daily schedule of anything, I'm hoping that the way these pages are structured will make it possible for you to pace yourself as you take the time to think about the day's message. Give yourself time to let it sink in. Find ways to apply it to your life as it happens and where possible; take the time to examine any of the resources included with various entries.

I've also included a few pages at the end of each day where you can take notes and reflect on how the day's lesson impacts you.

Seven Days to Higher Ground Day 1-This is where you begin...

Rather than start this devotional at January 1st, I've decided to start at Day 1. This made perfect sense to me because that's really where we should be starting, wherever day 1 happens to be for you. So, here goes:

John 5:8
Jesus said to him, "Rise, take up your bed and walk."

What better way to start a journey than by simply getting up and moving away from whatever it is that has held you back. No, I don't mean give up everything. Moving forward requires wisdom as well as courage. But the biggest thing is that once you have made the decision to make some necessary changes, you've got to take some action. Start a list, make a plan, find a trusted confidant to bounce some ideas off of, talk to a pastor, do something...just get going. A Whole new life awaits you if you can just trust that He has the power and the desire to make you new. He promises this in His word. Trust Him, get up and move forward.

_____

_____

_____

_____

_____

_____

_____

_____

_____

_____

_____

_____

_____

_____

_____

_____

_____

_____

_____

_____

_____

_____

_____

_____

_____

Day 2-Keep Swimming…

If you're reading this, smile. You're still moving forward. You are still focused on doing the thing. So, here is some useful advice:

2 Timothy 1:13
Hold fast the pattern of sound words in which you have heard from in faith and love which are Christ Jesus.

Reading the Bible can be intimidating. Especially if part of our struggle has been with feeling worthy of God's love and peace. But in order to have deeper understanding of God's word, we must continue to delve into it and diligently seek the meaning it holds. Study His word, find a concordance or Bible dictionary that you can use to look up terms that you don't understand. One of the most valuable tools I use is Nelson's Compact Bible Commentary. It breaks down each verse and explains what is going on. This is very useful in books of the Bible that are filled with metaphors and imagery such as Song of Solomon instead of the straightforward teaching of the Book of Proverbs.

_____

_____

_____

_____

_____

_____

_____

_____

_____

_____

_____

_____

_____

_____

_____

_____

_____

_____

_____

_____

_____

_____

_____

Day 3-Hump Day…

Whether it is Wednesday or not, getting to the third step of anything is a crucial point. This is where you decide whether or not the next day's efforts will be worth your time. I assure you; they will be. Especially if we're talking about taking the next steps toward solidifying your relationship with God. Keep going, you're doing great!

Ephesians 2:13
But now in Christ Jesus, you who once were far off have been brought near by the blood of Christ.

This is the point, exactly! The very fact that no matter how far away we once were, He can make us new and we can move closer and closer to Him. There is no sin great enough to separate you from the love of Christ. If you confess to Him and you accept Him as your Savior, He extends His hand and says, "Hold on, we're moving away from the person you once were. I'm making you new." There will be times when you feel discouraged, but these are part of the deal. It isn't all hearts and flowers. But it is all necessary to make you into the person He created you to be. This is exciting. Step to Him confidently and accept His grace.

_____

_____

_____

_____

_____

_____

_____

_____

_____

_____

_____

_____

_____

_____

_____

_____

_____

_____

_____

_____

_____

Day 4-Momentum

Step by step, that is how you will reach your goal. No matter where you're coming from, the point is that you remember that one day you'll look back at this time in your life and be thankful that you made the choice to keep moving forward.

Deuteronomy 6:18
Do what is right and good in the Lord's sight, so that it may go well with you and you may go in and take over the good land the Lord promised on oath to your ancestors.

Some days, this is the best you can hope for; to do what is right and good in the Lord's sight. Some days, this is more of a struggle than it should be. When you become a Christian, things don't automatically start to fall into place.

_____

_____

_____

_____

_____

_____

_____

_____

_____

_____

_____

_____

_____

_____

_____

_____

_____

_____

_____

_____

_____

_____

_____

_____

Day 5-Practice makes perfect…

"Daily walking close to Thee, let it be, dear Lord, let it be…"

From the hymn, Just a Closer Walk with Thee.

The words to this song offer comfort and inspiration. We all need this, whether we admit it or not. Nobody is perfect, nor will they ever be. If we persist in developing our relationship with Christ, we can get as close as possible. But the key is in persisting.

Hebrews 4:11
Let us therefore be diligent to enter that rest, lest anyone fall according to the same example of disobedience.

What does this mean exactly? It means that we must try our best every day to fix our eyes on Jesus and what He tried to teach so many years ago. If our focus is shifted away from all of our shortcomings and what we perceive to be our weaknesses or even our strengths, we can then focus on the strengths of Jesus and apply them to our everyday situations. When we do what Jesus would do, we are setting the best possible example and therefore bringing Him glory.

_____

_____

_____

_____

_____

_____

_____

_____

_____

_____

_____

_____

_____

_____

_____

_____

_____

_____

_____

_____

Day 6-Almost there...

Rounding out the first week of working through this devotional, be encouraged that you have almost reached your day of rest. On the seventh day, God rested and so should we. So, in preparation for that rest, let's take a look at what we've accomplished this week.

Genesis 2:1-2
Thus, the heavens and the earth were completed in all their vast array. By the seventh day God had finished the work he had been doing; so, on the seventh day he rested from all his work.

It is important to gently evaluate our efforts and to be satisfied that our work has been of an acceptable quality. Often, we go through the motions of our daily lives and we fail to see the significance of maintaining even the most mundane of routines. Although it may not seem we've done anything significant, the very act of living through the day and presenting ourselves a s capable and willing to keep moving is sometimes worthy of the greatest recognition. Give yourself credit for living a life that honors God. He is paying attention to the value we place on every moment He gives us.

_____

_____

_____

_____

_____

_____

_____

_____

_____

_____

_____

_____

_____

_____

_____

_____

_____

_____

_____

_____

_____

_____

_____

_____

Day 7-Reflection Time

We've reached the seventh day and from this point on, we'll be focusing on getting into God's word with the intent of giving Scripture a deeper context in our everyday lives.

Joshua 1:8
Keep this Book of the Law always on your lips; meditate on it day and night, so that you may be careful to do everything written in it. Then you will be prosperous and successful.

Reading God's word and knowing God's word are not necessarily the same thing, unless we consistently seek to make them the same in or hearts and minds. When we read the Scriptures, we must take in the words as though they are the very air that we breathe. We must allow God's word to give us life and to illuminate us from the inside out. As we read, we must consider not only the meaning of the text, but the backdrop against which it was written as well as who wrote it and why it was written.

_____

_____

_____

_____

_____

_____

_____

_____

_____

_____

_____

_____

_____

_____

_____

_____

_____

_____

_____

_____

_____

_____

_____

In Closing

As I stated at the beginning, this journey is lengthy and truthfully, is never really over. The key to success here is in holding onto the desire to live out the life that God planned for you. He will stand by you. Even when it seems like we are all alone, rest assured that He is with you, helping you through each challenging time.

Continue to study His word. Ask questions; seek out those who are knowledgeable; Pray for wisdom and discernment. Whatever you are seeking, He will help you find it. Break free from self-destructive patterns so that you can follow His leading.

This is just the beginning. If you need to review this devotional one hundred times, then do so. Some of the most helpful resources I've found, I've read more than five times. The Bible itself holds a new bit of wisdom for me every time I read a passage. He opens our minds and allows us to comprehend what we are able to handle knowing. It may seem overwhelming at times, but He will never give you more than you can deal with. Trust God first. Seek Him. Obey Him. Receive the blessings He has for you.

I pray that you find this resource useful and that you can use what you learn hereto not only receive His blessings, but to pour those blessings out into the lives of those you meet. This gift is a one size fits all. So, pass it on to anyone and everyone that you think might benefit from a closer walk with God.

I wish you continued success on your journey, and I can't wait to meet you on the other side.

God bless you.

Other titles from Higher Ground Books & Media:

Wise Up to Rise Up by Rebecca Benston

A Path to Shalom by Steen Burke

For His Eyes Only by John Salmon, Ph.D.

Miracles: I Love Them by Forest Godin

32 Days with Christ's Passion by Mark Etter

Knowing Affliction and Doing Recovery by John Baldasare

Out of Darkness by Stephen Bowman

Breaking the Cycle by Willie Deeanjlo White

Healing in God's Power by Yvonne Green

Chronicles of a Spiritual Journey by Stephen Shepherd

The Real Prison Diaries by Judy Frisby

My Name is Sam…And Heaven is Still Shining Through by Joe Siccardi

Add these titles to your collection today!

http://www.highergroundbooksandmedia.com

Do you have a story to tell?

Higher Ground Books & Media is an independent Christian-based publisher specializing in stories of triumph! Our purpose is to empower, inspire, and educate through the sharing of personal experiences.

Please visit our website for our submission guidelines.

http://www.highergroundbooksandmedia.com